What Is Sanctification?

What Is Sanctification?

by

Leslie Parrott

Beacon Hill Press of Kansas City
Kansas City, Missouri

First Printing, 1952
Revised, 1979

ISBN: 0-8341-0077-0

Printed in
the United States of America

25 24 23 22 21 20

Contents

Preface

Though sanctification is the distinguishing doctrine of our church, there are many sincere people in our congregations fighting carnality in their lives. Seemingly, they have not grasped God's plan for "purity and power."

To help these people, I have written from this point of view—that the reader knows nothing about sanctification. Imagining myself absolutely ignorant on holiness, I have asked all the questions that would come into my mind. I realize the publishers have given us many more scholarly discussions on sanctification, but in these pages I have tried to give simple answers to these elementary questions.

Since the major part of this material has come from my own experience, my acknowledgements go to many who have knowingly or unknowingly contributed to this manuscript by their testimony or conduct.

I am especially indebted to Richard Taylor for help in defining carnality; to General Superintendent Hardy C. Powers for wise counsel; and to my parents, Dr. and Mrs. A. L. Parrott, who by their Christian example during my struggle for sanctification held me to the fact that holiness can be lived.

—LESLIE PARROTT

Salem, Oregon
1949

A New Preface

More than 30 years ago I received the Holy Spirit into my life in His sanctifying power. It had not been easy for me, because I was hung-up on the dilemma of contradiction between holiness theology and holiness experience. I was especially bothered by the inconsistencies of Christians I knew who professed to be sanctified and the theological concept of eradication.

Finally, one night in the little second floor apartment near Willamette University, Salem, Ore., where I was a graduate student, I was on my knees praying with the Bible open before me on the bed, the pages dampened by my tears. In the depths of my spiritual frustration I finally cried out, "Dear Lord, If there is no one in the church who is sanctified, I still believe the experience is taught in the New Testament and I want to be entirely sanctified, right now."

That night, God the Holy Spirit came into my life in a way I have never forgotten and with a Presence that has been real with me until now. Spiritual victory in my life is dated from the time God sanctified me entirely instead of the time of my conversion. This may be partially because I was saved in childhood and never indulged in the popular vices. Spiritual defeat in my life came from the sins of the spirit, not the passions of the flesh. It was at the time I was sanctified entirely that the problems of resentment, self-pity, negativism, and other manifestations of the sinful nature within me were translated into a great new life in the Spirit, as carnality (the condition of sin in the will) was eradicated and a new Presence took over.

Out of my joy in the marvelous new life, I wrote, *What Is Sanctification?* hoping to help others experience this same grace in the Holy Spirit.

And now, after 14 printings I have been requested to edit the manuscript for a new edition. I am now a much more experienced writer and I hope a better one. If I were writing this manuscript again from scratch, I am sure I would use many less quotation marks and commas. And I am sure I would change *folks* to *people* and would do away with the contractions. But since there is something about the vitality of my feelings that come through with the youthful style of expression, I have decided not to tamper with what I wrote in 1949.

However, after all these years there is no thought of changing the content of these pages. I still believe in and have experienced entire sanctification as I have described it in these pages. I understand the theology better now and the experience has been tested and proven in ways I never expected. But it is the same theology and the same experience now as it was then.

So, here is the manuscript just as I wrote it in longhand more than 30 years ago. I commend these pages to you with a prayer that you may know the joy of His Presence fully.

—LESLIE PARROTT

Olivet Nazarene College
Kankakee, Illinois
February 2, 1979

Introduction

One reason the message of holiness has lived is due to the fact that its advocates have been prolific writers. The glorious experience of entire sanctification is invariably accompanied by an insatiable desire to tell others the glad news of this spiritual deliverance.

The generation immediately past produced many capable writers on this theme. Today, it augurs well for the future of the message and the movement to find men, such as the author of this manuscript, taking up this important task.

The author has many qualifications which would indicate that the reader's time will be well spent in perusing these pages; but, most important of all, I know the truths contained in this message have been hammered out on the anvil of Leslie Parrott's own experience.

I commend this book to all who are interested in the Canaan-land of perfect love.

—HARDY C. POWERS
General Superintendent, Church of the Nazarene, 1944-68

Dallas, Tex.
1950

"He [Paul] said unto them, Have ye received the Holy Ghost since ye believed? And they [the Ephesians] said unto him, We have not so much as heard whether there be any Holy Ghost." "Sanctify them through thy truth: thy word is truth." "Ye shall know the truth and the truth shall make you free" (Acts 19:2; John 17:17; John 8:32).

1

What Is Meant by the Term "Sanctification"?

Bible students know that "sanctification" is scriptural. The words *sanctify, sanctified,* or *sanctification* have been used 164 times in the Word of God. In the Old Testament, things were sanctified. Mount Sinai, where the laws of Moses were given, was sanctified. The seventh day was sanctified. The altar in the Temple and the Temple itself were sanctified.

In the New Testament we read that Christ died for our sanctification. "Wherefore Jesus also, that he might sanctify the people with his own blood, suffered without the gate" (Heb. 13:12). Not only did Christ suffer for our cleansing, but He impressed upon His followers the urgency of sanctification. In His last prayer with them prior to the Crucifixion, He pleaded with His Father: "I pray not that thou shouldest take them out of the world, but that thou shouldest keep them from the evil. They are not of the world, even as I am not of the world. Sanctify them through thy truth: thy word is truth" (John 17:15-17). The ultimate purpose of Christ's death was that His believers might be sanctified.

Now we come to the question, "What do you mean by the term *sanctification?*" On my first day as a freshman college student, our rhetoric professor told us that, in order to get the most from our education, we should buy a good dictionary. After standing in line, I walked out of the college bookstore with a Webster's dictionary under my arm. Since then I've looked upon that volume as an authority on words. Everyone else accepted it as such; so did I.

When I turned to the dictionary for a definition of the word *sanctify,* I found this: "Sanctify is a transitive verb that means to make holy, cleanse from impurity, pollution, or sin." Added significance is given this definition when we realize that it was not written by a "holiness theologian" but by a scholar whose sole interest was in defining the term. Since a transitive verb connotes action that changes something, a person who is sanctified by the Holy Spirit is different than he was before he was sanctified.

Throughout Christ's teachings and especially in the Sermon on the Mount, He taught that salvation was twofold. The antagonism He aroused in the scribes and Pharisees on this point helped cause His crucifixion. They considered themselves the "religious aristocracy" of their day, and still Jesus said: "Except your righteousness shall exceed the righteousness of the scribes and Pharisees, ye shall in no case enter into the kingdom of heaven" (Matt. 5:20). These people were church members who attended regularly. They had definite hours of the day when they went into the Temple to pray. They fasted certain days of the week. They were far more strict in keeping the Sabbath than the average Christian today. What's wrong? Their righteousness was all external. They had the outward manifestations of goodness, but their hearts were black. There must be the outward demonstration of righteousness, but Christ demands an inward change. "Ye must be born again."

Just as salvation is twofold, so is sin. There are the visible acts: stealing, lying, blaspheming, etc. Those sins are forgiven in regeneration; but there is still an inward condition that "leans toward sinning." That is dealt with in sanctification. You may be forgiven for your acts of sin, but not for the condition of sin in your heart; it must be cleansed. You may be forgiven for lying, but not for the deceitful spirit that made you want to lie; it must be cleansed. You may be forgiven for the cutting words you spoke, but not for the unreasonable prejudices which made you say those things; they must be cleansed. Christ forgives sins, but He cleanses the condition of sin in the heart.

Sanctification is really the completion of the work begun in regeneration. John Wesley spoke of those who had been saved and not sanctified as "merely justified." "As yet," he said, "they have not gone on for all that the Lord has for them." This was not an effort by Wesley to put down the experience of the new birth, but to emphasize the further work of heart cleansing.

The person who has been saved and then faces light on sanctification sings:

Lord Jesus, I long to be *perfectly whole.*
I want Thee *forever to dwell in my soul.*
Break down *every idol;* cast out *every foe.*
Now wash me, and *I shall be whiter than
    snow.*

The person who is saved, but refuses to walk into the experience of sanctification, should sing:

Lord Jesus, I long to be *partially whole.*
I want Thee *part of the time to dwell in my
    soul.*
Break down a *few idols;* cast out a *few foes.*
Wash me a little, and I'll be *some whiter
    than before.*

There have been many standards of holiness preached. Some say, "If you slam the door, kick the cat, and speak mean to your wife, you are not sanctified." Of course! But that is not all the truth. I know some folks who have never been saved who wouldn't do those things. That is a matter of being "a lady or a gentleman." There are people who by their very nature never seem to get "ruffled" or "upset." They are soft-spoken and agreeable but make no profession of religion.

There are those who say that the sanctified will dress modestly as becomes a Christian. True enough! However, there is a lady in our neighborhood who wears black stockings, long hair, no cosmetics, and no jewelry. She runs a fruit stand seven days a week, making no attempt to attend church, and can swear like a drunken sailor at

14

anyone who upsets a box of peaches. We could scarcely call her sanctified.

Then some say that a sanctified person will be loyal to his church by regular attendance and by tithing. That is true; but the Mormons who never smoke, never drink coffee, tea, or liquor, and who attend church regularly, always paying their tithe, would be insulted if we called them "holiness folks."

Sanctification goes farther than the external. It is more deeply rooted than the dress, the mannerisms, or the conduct. Sanctification is centered in the heart. The test of sanctification, then, is more than the slamming of doors, the length of the skirt, and the paying of tithes. The test is: Do I exemplify Christ in my spirit, my attitudes, and my motives? I'm sure you have seen some adult rebuke an adolescent when the spirit the elder showed was far worse than the misdemeanor of the youngster. Sanctification takes away that critical spirit, that lazy attitude, the wrong motive, the ugly character, and deposits in its place the spirit of divine love.

In summary: Sanctification is a heart cleansing of the condition which lends itself to acts that hurt the soul and the kingdom of Christ. Once the heart is pure, this Spirit of Christ comes in to dwell in His fullness.

Be not deceived; the sanctified person is not now to sit down and coast to heaven. He is cleansed and filled with the Spirit, that he may begin to grow in grace. But we'll deal with that subject under another question.

2

Is Sanctification Necessary?

Jesus thought sanctification was necessary for His disciples. If the Church today were to appoint eleven laymen, commissioning them with the full responsibility of Christianity for the world, we would declare the act preposterous. Scorning the idea, we'd say, "It's absurd to think that eleven men could evangelize today's world." I agree. However, it is no more ridiculous for the Church today to lay "world evangelism" on the shoulders of eleven men than for Christ to call out a handful of fishermen and send them into all the world to preach the gospel to every creature. He knew they were not ready to go. First, He said, "tarry ye in the city of Jerusalem, until ye be endued with power from on high" (Luke 24:49).

After Jesus had traveled all day, preaching and teaching, He and His disciples approached a little village. Being unusually weary, He asked the disciples to go ahead into the village and get food and shelter for the night, while He rested on the outskirts of the town. Soon they came scurrying back. Even in the distance, He could see the dust eddying around their rushing feet. He saw them talking excitedly and gesticulating wildly. Arriving out of breath, they besieged the Master with their story. Peter no doubt did most of the talking. "Master, we told them in the village that You had come, wanting food and shelter. We expected hospitality, but instead they refused us any consideration and said in no uncertain terms that we were unwelcome in their town." Then amid loud clamoring and violent waving of arms, each in his own way said, "Lord, it's not right; You should call down fire out of heaven and burn up the whole village." Jesus' sharp rebuke put them to shame.

There Jesus was reminded again that His followers weren't ready to evangelize the world. What if the disciples had possessed the power and had called down fire to consume the town? The news would have spread abroad, and not one would have listened further to "the mad maniacs who burn up unrepentant towns." Christ knew that spirit of vengeful anger had to be cleansed.

On another occasion the sons of thunder, James and John, showed a selfish motive in courting special appointments by the Master. Christ knew "the repulsive egotism" of His messengers must be eradicated.

On occasion, all the disciples had shown fear and unwillingness to witness for Jesus. That fear, He knew must be supplanted with "divine moral courage."

Too, the Lord possessed foreknowledge. He could see years ahead in the lives of the apostles. They would face discouragements, persecutions, and martyrdom. And unless they had that "power from on high," Christ knew they would desert to easier occupations.

There, Jesus "commanded them that they should not depart from Jerusalem, but wait for the promise of the Father. . . . But ye shall receive power, after that the Holy Ghost is come upon you" (Acts 1:4, 8). Those disciples weren't to evangelize their Jerusalem neighborhood until, first, they tarried for power. Therefore, if sanctification was necessary for those men in the unhurried world of 2,000 years ago, then it is certainly necessary for you and me in the 20th century.

Also, sanctification is necessary for victorious living. Jesus, in the 17th chapter of John, refused to pray for His disciples to be sheltered from the evil of the world. He prayed that they might be sanctified, and thereby live victoriously in a sinful world.

Some Christians eke out an existence without any real joy or exuberance. Christianity is, to them, a mere "insurance policy" against hell. They have no vibrant testimony and bear no Christian fruit. God never intended that kind of life for us. He wants us to possess some spiritual enthusiasm, and a joy in our hearts that sets us apart from the world. Our lives must count for Him.

When I was in the seventh grade, a craze for making crystal radio sets swept our part of the country. Infatuated with the idea, three of us boys pooled our assets, visited the junk shop and the dime store, in accumulating the proper parts for making a set. Several evenings after school we tinkered with the idea until finally it materialized. I well remember the time I pulled those earphones down against my ears as I slowly turned the needle. The machine crackled, sputtered, and spit; faded in and faded out, and seemed alive with static. I couldn't hear the speaking, but I could hear the music from radio station WTAX, six blocks down the street from our house.

Imagine that before us now we have that crystal set and by its side the best modern radio that money can buy. As we listen to the crystal set, the reception is poor and often there is none. However, turning the dial of the modern radio, in a moment we have 50 radio stations with such power that the tone must be lowered to save bursting our eardrums. What is the difference? The transmitter is the same in both instances, and their source of power is identical. Obviously the difference is in the two machines.

You need not live a "crystal-set" life of mediocre Christianity. Christ will provide you with a rich, full life that is a vibrant testimony to the power of God.

Too, sanctification is necessary for unity. Would Christ want to come back to the world and find the churches bickering among themselves over little issues? Would He want to find church leaders striving for position? Would He want to find unseemly conduct on the part of church members? No! He has a better plan. "And the very God of peace sanctify you wholly; and I pray God your whole spirit and soul and body be preserved blameless unto the coming of our Lord Jesus Christ" (1 Thess. 5:23). No crisis you cannot meet will ever come to your life if only you have the comparable inner resources. That inner resource is "the fulness of Christ."

In summary: Sanctification is not a luxury that may be either accepted or rejected with little consideration. It is absolutely necessary for a victorious, fruitful Christian testimony.

3

How Do I Get Sanctified?

This chapter is brief, for the uncomplicated steps to sanctification are explicit. Since "entire sanctification" begins with regeneration, let's make that our starting point.

There are two definite steps in "regeneration," first of which is *repentance*. This means a recognition of your sins, but more than that—a godly sorrow for your sinful acts. God hears no prayer for forgiveness which does not come from a contrite spirit. Repentance also means "confession"; not a harboring of sins, but an outright confession of them to God. Then, repentance means "forsaking of sin." The pentitent soul does not reach for God with one arm while clutching the world with the other. He turns his back on sinful acts, habits, and companions to give full attention to serving God.

Once we have repented of sins, then in simple faith we trust Christ for salvation. We are now justified in God's sight, regenerated in our own souls, saved from eternal punishment, and saved to a life of service and a heavenly home.

Then there comes a time in the life of every "believer" when he feels the need for a deeper work in his heart. By repentance and faith, our sins have already disappeared in the sea of God's forgetfulness. But the good things still remain in our lives.

Now we are ready to begin our consecration. We pray: "Lord, I have little talent, but such as I have is Thine. I have few financial assets; but, Lord, what I do have is Yours. My time, my family, my job, my future, myself—all I am and ever hope to be is fully Yours. Lord, take me as I am. Cleanse me and fill me with Thy Holy Spirit." After we have made the last bit of consecration to God, we, through faith in His power, believe that He accepts the gift and now sanctifies wholly.

To clarify further, let me outline the process.

I. Regeneration

    A. Consciousness of a personal need for salvation

    B. Repentance
    This includes:
        1. Godly sorrow for your sins
        2. Confessing your sins
        3. Forsaking your sins

    C. Faith (believing that God can and does do the work now)

    D. The result, regeneration

II. Entire sanctification

    A. Consciousness of a personal need for sanctification

    B. Consecration
    This includes:
        1. The past
        2. The present

3. The future
C. Faith (believing that God can and does sanctify now)
D. The result, entire sanctification

To clarify still further, I illustrate: Visualize two small stacks of books before you, which represent your life. One stack represents the sins in your life; the other, the virtues. To be saved you begin with the stack of books which represents your sins. One after another in the process of repentance, place the books upon the altar, until all sins are confessed and all books are on the altar. After repentance is completed, trust Christ for salvation. "If we confess our sins, he is faithful and just to forgive us our sins, and to cleanse us from all unrighteousness" (1 John 1:9). Thus through repentance and faith, the stack of books representing your sins is taken away. You are justified.

Then there comes a time when you feel the need of sanctification in your heart. The other stack of books, which represents the "good things" in your life, is still left. One by one you lay those books upon the altar in consecration until finally the last thing is consecrated and the last book is on the altar. You are wholly in God's hands. Then by faith believe that God does the work of "entire sanctification."

I know no simpler way of expressing it than this: You are saved by repentance and faith. You are sanctified by consecration and faith.

For you who have a struggle over faith, let me give you the experience of a friend. For years he had been a struggling seeker after "holiness." In sincerity and conduct there was no one in the congregation more conscientious than he. But his usefulness was hindered by his lack of victory in sanctification. Again and again he had consecrated himself to God, but he could not believe that the "cleansing" was done.

At the close of a Sunday morning service, he came to the altar again to seek sanctification. The few who prayed with him did not remain long, for they all said, "Poor Homer, he comes every time an invitation is given." Soon the church was deserted except for my friend and his pastor. They prayed until after 1 p.m.

Finally the minister said, "Homer, if you are positive that you are wholly consecrated and in no way are holding back from God, then drive a mental stake here at this altar and trust God for sanctification. Every time the devil accuses you of not being sanctified, point to this mental stake and say, 'There I consecrated myself to God for sanctification. I have not taken back any part of my consecration. So, if I'm not sanctified, it's God's fault.'" A glint came in his eye as Homer caught the significance of what the pastor had said. It's been several years since my friend drove that mental stake, but till now the Lord has honored his faith with the witness to sanctification.

Sanctification is not for a few of God's chosen saints. It is the normal Christian life God has provided for His children. Today, if you know you're saved, consecrate yourself wholly to Christ, and then trust God for "entire sanctification."

4

When Do I Get Sanctified?

Every denomination believes in some form of sanctification. Our Catholic friends believe we are cleansed in purgatory. I know some good folks who believe that we are saved and sanctified all at once. Others think we are saved and then begin the long process of growing into the experience of sanctification. Some think we are sanctified just before death, and still other believe glorification and sanctification are synonymous. You are no doubt an intelligent, thinking person; and since there are some loopholes in almost any argument (theological or otherwise), I'll merely give the scripture and you may be your own judge.

Acts 19:2: "Have ye received the Holy Ghost since ye believed? And they said unto him, We have not so much as heard whether there be any Holy Ghost."

I quoted this verse once and a man said, "Don't you know the *Revised Standard Version* says 'when ye believed' instead of 'since ye believed'?" He's right. It does say that. But I don't think it changes the meaning of the verse, for in both instances the answer was no. They had believed on Christ but had not received the baptism of the Holy Ghost.

Acts 8:14-17: "Now when the apostles which were at Jerusalem heard that Samaria had received the word of God, they sent unto them Peter and John: who, when they were come down, prayed for them, that they might receive the Holy Ghost: (for as yet he was fallen upon none of them: only they were baptized in the name of the Lord Jesus.) Then laid they their hands on them, and they received the Holy Ghost."

As soon as the mother church in Jerusalem heard that the people of Samaria had received "the word," they dispatched two of their best evangelists, Peter and John, to go preach to them on the Holy Ghost. "For as yet he was fallen upon none of them."

Acts 10:1-4: "There was a certain man in Caesarea called Cornelius, a centurion of the band called the Italian band, a devout man, and one that feared God with all his house, which gave much alms to the people, and prayed to God alway. He saw in a vision evidently about the ninth hour of the day an angel of God coming in to him, and saying unto him, Cornelius. And when he looked on him, he was afraid, and said, What is it, Lord? And he said unto him, Thy prayers and thine alms are come up for a memorial before God."

I wish our churches today could be filled with people equaling this description. Notice:

1. A devout man;
2. One that feared God;

3. With all his house (He evidently won his family.);

4. Which gave much alms (He no doubt paid his tithe.);

5. And prayed to God alway;

6. God sent a special messenger down to tell him that his prayers had come up as a memorial before God.

But as you read on in this chapter, you see that Cornelius felt a need for a deeper work in his heart. He sent to Joppa down by the sea where Peter was vacationing, and asked him to come and minister to his household. Peter came. And in the 44th verse of the chapter, the climax is reached when it says, "While Peter yet spake these words, the Holy Ghost fell on all them which heard the word."

In John 17:9-17, Christ prays, "not for the world," but that His disciples might be sanctified. In Ephesians, the fifth chapter, we are told that Christ gave himself that "the church" might be sanctified.

We will not argue the question; you be the judge. But it seems to me that any objective interpretation of the Scriptures teaches that we are sanctified as a second definite work of grace.

5

What Will Sanctification Do for Me?

In my own experience, the spiritual struggle over sanctification was seated in eradication. I knew I was saved. I was consecrated, and I longed for a life of Christian service. I know now I was wrong in my approach; but as I examined my own life, and as I observed the lives of other "self-professed" sanctified folks, I doubted eradication.

Having sought the counsel of several whom I trusted, I was more confused than ever. I read widely on sanctification but found very little on eradication. What I did find was wrapped in such folds of "theological jargon" that I found difficulty in applying it to my life.

Although I could not testify to "complete cleansing," I found less satisfaction in alternative doctrines; their fallacies were glaring.

Over the period of a year, I wrestled with this problem until finally I fell before God praying, "Lord, there must be such a thing as heart cleansing. There is no other answer to the problem of sin. I can't understand how it works, but I'm ready; sanctify me now." I had many times gone through my consecration, but I had tried to find "rest" in a Spirit-filled life without eradication. But on that day when I cried, "Cleanse me now," the Lord wrought a change in my heart that has been reflected in my spirit and attitude from then till now.

At the time I was sanctified, I squelched an intellectual curiosity about eradication, and was reconciled to living my life, never understanding it. However, when my heart was right, I soon "thought my way clear" on "cleansing." It came in these four steps.

1. I determined to find an answer to the question, "What is carnality?"

Carnality is not in your physical—the flesh. If so, you would be less sinful with your leg amputated, and you would be wholly pure when your body was cremated. Carnality has nothing to do with your humanity. It is a soul condition which affects your motives, attitudes, and affections. It is like a "spot on the lungs" or an "ulcer in the stomach." As a condition it may be removed, but when the right causes are present, the condition may return.

Before I was sanctified, I tried to make myself believe that it would be impossible to sin if carnality were removed. This fallacy is evident. It is no more reasonable to believe this than to believe that, once cured of a disease, we have an eternal security against its return. Pneumonia will return the second or third time if we allow our physical condition to "run down" and then expose ourselves to the proper germs.

Richard Taylor says, "Eradication does not always mean a tone of voice, or facial expression. But the delinquency is not due to a lack of Christlikeness in spirit or motive but a lack of Christlikeness in understanding and emotional balance. The carnal nature is simply a bloated self, a self nature that has become enlarged and distorted, an enlarged sense of one's importance, a desire to have self honored, a hypersensitiveness to injuries, a tendency to magnify the faults of others, self-willed."

In brief, carnality is unsanctified self: self-love, self-seeking and self-will.

2. The second step in "thinking through" eradication is: "Is God able to cleanse from all sin?"

Calvinism says that Christ can save from the result of sin but not from sin. If the sinner sins, he is damned; if the Christian sins, he is taken to heaven. This unmistakably limits the power of God. If an omnipotent God can forgive sins, He can cleanse sin.

Our same Calvinistic brethren say that we must sin every day in thought, word, and deed. This again limits God's power. If He can save us from the grosser sins, then He can save us from all sin. Only the most prejudiced trend of thought will say that a God who can create a human soul does not have the power to cleanse that same soul from the sin in which it has become degraded.

3. Next: "Is eradication scriptural?"

Here there is no stronger word than God's Word.

Romans 8:7-8: "Because the carnal mind is enmity against God: for it is not subject to the law of God, neither indeed can be. So then they that are in the flesh cannot please God."

Since the carnal mind "is enmity" against the law of God, and since the law of God is "love," then to harmonize the soul with the law of love, carnality must be eradicated. Love cannot be legislated. It must come from the heart. Therefore, divine love must come from a pure heart.

Acts 15:8-9: "And God, which knoweth the hearts, bare them witness, giving them the Holy Ghost, even as he did unto us; and put no difference between us and them, purifying their hearts by faith."

In these two verses Peter concludes that the cleansing by the Holy Spirit may be universally appropriated, no one being excepted.

Other fortifying scriptures are: Matt. 3:11-12; Jas. 4:8; Rom. 6:1-2; 8:1-13; 1 John 1:9.

4. The last step in "thinking through" on eradication is: "Determine not to judge the doctrine by the lives of people."

I know many whom I believe consistently live the sanctified life, but every time I've set my eyes upon people, I've been disappointed. However, if every person professing sanctification were a hypocrite and were finally cast into hell, it would not change God's Word one iota. Christian perfection is not an ideal. It is the normal stratum of victorious experience, attainable and livable now. But don't be tricked by Satan into watching the fallacies of others.

In summary, I thought my way clear on eradication by these four steps:

1. What is carnality?
2. Is God able to cleanse the heart?
3. Is eradication scriptural?
4. Determine not to judge the doctrine by the lives of people.

Not only will sanctification cleanse the heart, but it will give spiritual power to your life. Salvation is attractive. People may be condemned for their sins in your presence; but if you live the sanctified life, they'll say, "If ever I get religion I want it just like so-and-so."

I have a friend who held a revival in an isolated community in Texas many years ago. An old fellow affectionately known as Uncle Pink arranged for the meeting, which was held in a tabernacle built for the purpose. There was no music and none of the advertising we feel necessary for a revival. But at the end of the five-day meeting (which did not include a Sunday) 185 persons had knelt at the improvised altar.

Checking into the situation, my friend found that for 20 years Uncle Pink had lived a good sanctified life in that community. He swapped horses and exchanged work with all the men of the neighborhood until they all knew him intimately. When he was ready for the revival meeting, they helped him build the tabernacle and then they all came to the meeting praying, "Lord, give me what Uncle Pink's got."

When the Lord sanctifies, He cleanses the heart and gives a power in your life that is an attraction to the cause of Christ.

6

What Will Sanctification *Not* Do for Me?

1. Sanctification will not destroy your free moral agency.

You are born with a free will. You can will to serve or not to serve God. You may choose evil or good, righteousness or sin. At no time in this life will that free will be destroyed.

I have little patience with the doctrine which says you may be eternally saved and then live licentiously. God will sustain His grace in your heart as long as your will cooperates with Him. It is not probable, but possible, that after you have been sanctified a half century you could set yourself against God and go into willful transgression. Sanctification will not destroy your free moral agency.

2. Sanctification will not place you beyond temptation.

The devil doesn't die the day you are sanctified. The thief doesn't break into the hovel. Instead, he robs the castle. Though your temptations will take on a new form, they will be as real and as consistent after the experience of heart cleansing as before. (We will deal with these temptations in another chapter.)

3. Sanctification will not destroy your humanity.

No mortal will reach the realm of "human perfection." Sanctification deals with the heart, not the flesh. If your hair is red, sanctification will not change its color. A Scotchman will still be Scotch and a poor man will still be poor even after they are sanctified.

4. Sanctification will not make you a mature Christian.

Young people, especially, are tricked by Satan to believe that the Lord in His sanctifying power will give them an experience equal to that of some saint who has walked with God for 50 years. No! You are cleansed that you may begin to grow in grace and become more Christlike in manner as the years proceed.

5. Sanctification will not make us all uniform.

If an agent of the government were to walk into your Sunday morning service and begin passing out $1,000 bills to everyone present, no two people would act the same on receiving theirs. Some would laugh; some, cry; some, run for the exit; and some would sit in their seats with no particular emotional reaction.

Everyone cannot be poured into one mold. An old gentleman in my congregation used to cause me unending strain because he expected everyone who sought and claimed sanctification to react emotionally as he did when he was sanctified. We are all created different. We don't see things from the same point of view. And not even sanctification will make us alike in this life.

7

What Will Happen to the Unsanctified on the Day of Judgment?

This question caused me difficulty because I knew of a thief who hanged there on a cross by the side of Christ. In the last moments of his life he cried, "Lord, remember me when thou comest into thy kingdom." And Jesus said, "To day shalt thou be with me in paradise." By any accepted sense of time, the thief didn't get sanctified; but I'm sure you and I, both, expect to see him in heaven.

Also, I know of individuals who were saved on their deathbeds. I expect to see them in heaven; but, by my understanding of time, they were not sanctified. "Still," I reasoned, "God has but one standard on which we'll all be judged." I thought on this for some time before I finally got a satisfactory solution. My answer hasn't come from a theology book, but it is sound doctrine.

We are born into this world under the grace of

God. Should we die before we reach the age of accountability, our souls would be saved.

After we reach that age when we know the difference between sin and righteousness, we become accountable for our sins. The longer we live in sin, the deeper and more involved we become until that day we yield our hearts to God for salvation. After we are saved, we are once more under the grace of God.

Then there comes that time when we feel a need for a deeper work in our hearts. We are then sanctified. But even after we are sanctified, the Lord, from time to time, gives us new light. We are expected to walk in all His light. And at the judgment we'll be held in account for the amount of light we've had in our lives.

I'm not so concerned about these unusual cases like the thief on the cross. I'm perplexed about professing Christians who are walking back of light and are satisfied in their spiritual laziness, critical spirit, ugly attitudes, and selfish motives. On "God's Day of Reckoning," they will be judged on the light they spurned and on the Christian character they might have attained.

"And these things write we unto you, that your joy may be full. This then is the message which we have heard of him, and declare unto you, that God is light, and in him is no darkness at all. If we say that we have fellowship with him, and walk in darkness, we lie, and do not the truth: but if we walk in the light, as he is in the light, we have fellowship one with another, and the blood of Jesus Christ his Son cleanseth us from all sin" (1 John 1:4-7).

8

What Are the Temptations to the Sanctified?

1. We are tempted on the "loss of feeling."

One of Satan's best weapons concerns the matter of "feelings." He slyly begins with the broad accusation, "You don't feel right." It's true, emotion generally accompanies the witness of the spirit to cleansing; but we are foolish to expect "any certain feeling." God has made no promise of feeling in connection with the experience of sanctification; so we may know that we have fallen prey to the tricks of the devil if we begin to worry about "not feeling right."

Then Satan beguiles, "You don't feel as others say they do." That's a subtle approach, for Satan knows we humans (especially in youth) are hero worshipers. If a saint whom we admire testifies to some particular "feeling," then the tempter whispers, "You must not be sanctified because you don't feel like that." Nonsense! We're not built the same; so our emotional reactions can never be identical.

The devil continues, "You don't feel as you

formerly did." At the moment of cleansing, an emotional ecstasy, not necessarily but often, is enjoyed. This may last a few moments or a number of weeks. But eventually we settle down to the workday of a Christian soldier. There's a "deep, settled peace" in our hearts, but the emotional ecstasy is gone. Are we backslidden? Only the most senseless reasoning could reach that conclusion.

Remember: We're saved by faith, sanctified by faith, and kept by faith. Keep faithful and let the Lord be concerned with the "feeling."

2. We are tempted to compromise on terms.

A pastor of another denomination recently told me, "I believe what you preach, but I don't like the terms you use such as *eradication, perfection,* and *sanctification.*" The Holy Spirit makes us broad-minded, not narrow and bigoted. However, I don't think we should compromise on the name of the experience Christ called "sanctification," any more than we should compromise the expression "born again."

If compromising the terms *eradication* and *sanctification* is further to enlighten unfamiliar minds, then it may have some merit. But if our substitution is to lessen the reproach, our motive is wrong. Satan is so subtle in his approach that we may, without realizing it, grieve the Holy Spirit by compromising on terms.

3. We are tempted to compromise in methods.

The devil says, "Why don't you compromise just a little to prove to your unsaved friends that you are not out of date?"

A lady in a Western town told me that she planned to win her unsaved husband and family by compromising on some of the things they wanted to do, with the promise that the family would later attend church with her. She kept her word by indulging in their worldly amusements, but they all found excuses not to attend church when the time came. Within a year the "compromising Christian lady" had completely failed the means of grace and had become an enthusiastic accomplice to the worldly ways of the family. Spiritual compromise brings no gain, but evil. The world gives far more respect to the Christian who stands firm on his convictions than to the person who compromises to "go with the crowd."

4. We are tempted on spiritual pride.

If the devil can't get you to compromise, he'll then attack with a weapon just as devastating to the kingdom of God, "spiritual pride." There is nothing more repulsive to a sinner than a person exhibiting "self-righteousness." Throughout His ministry, Christ rebuked every evidence of self-exaltation. When the Pharisee and the publican entered the Temple to pray, the Pharisee with his haughty spirit began, "God, I thank thee, that I am not as other men are, extortioners, unjust, adulterers, or even as this publican. I fast twice in the week, I give tithes of all that I possess." God didn't hear the prayer of this self-righteous Pharisee, but He justified the publican who prayed seven words, "God be merciful to me a sinner."

I knew a student who fasted a certain day of each week in a room of the administration building where he could look down on the students marching into the dining hall. He said to himself, "If they were as religious as I am, they'd be fasting too." He told me that he held that haughty attitude until it ruined his Christian usefulness and he had to ask God to forgive him for his spiritual pride.

Another man told me, "I was so anxious to be humble that I actually became proud of my humility."

The sanctified person has nothing of which to be proud. Our cleansing is by the mercy and grace of God. Our unworthiness, our mistakes, and our blunders should be enough to keep away spiritual pride forever.

5. We are tempted to be impatient with others.

During a revival in our church, a middle-aged lady and her son were so remarkably saved that it brought rejoicing throughout the congregation. However, a few weeks later we narrowly escaped a rift in the church when the lady appeared at a church function dressed in more worldly fashion than the rest. Our group had not learned the lesson of patience with others. The light we had was yet darkness to the new convert.

Don't be tempted to discount the spiritual stature of others because they do not at the moment measure up to your convictions and impressions. In our efforts to hold the line on purity, we can become obnoxious. "Love suffereth long, and is kind."

6. We are tempted on misguided zeal.

In his letter to the Romans, Paul speaks of "a

zeal of God, but not according to knowledge." A backwoods preacher spoke of the third blessing of good sense. Contagious enthusiasm is a most desirable trait, but misguided zeal invariably leads to fanaticism. The main line is love out of a pure heart.

7. We are tempted to mistake light for guilt.

Not light but walking against light brings guilt. No one is expected to do what he doesn't know is his duty, nor is he condemned for what he hasn't known. "This is the condemnation, that light is come . . . and men loved darkness rather than light" (John 3:19). Don't be condemned over receiving light; for, "If we walk in the light, as he in the light, we have fellowship one with another, and the blood of Jesus Christ his Son cleanseth us from all sin." After we are sanctified, the Holy Spirit continues to give light in our lives. We are not guilty for receiving the light, but we are to cherish it and be obedient to its direction.

One word of caution: The light you receive may not be universal. God often deals with us individually. Therefore, don't be too hard on your brother who has not received the light you have.

8. We are tempted to rest in past experiences

We have put so much emphasis on the two crucial religious experiences that many have come to feel that sanctification is an end in itself. The complacent one prays, "Thank Thee, Lord, for completing all Thy work in my heart. I'll spend the rest of my life basking in Thy love." God does the cleansing work that we might be fit to enter the warfare against evil and for Christ.

Nor is there less guilt in resting on past victories. When a general reported a victory to Napoleon, he immediately asked, "What did you do the next day?" Our Christian life is progressive, with each past victory a mere stepping-stone to greater successes. Don't be tempted by Satan to live in past experiences.

In summary: You may expect severe tests and temptations after you are sanctified, as you did before. But be strong in the Lord; for, "There hath no temptation taken you but such as is common to man: but God is faithful who will not suffer you to be tempted above that ye are able; but will with the temptation also make a way to escape, that ye may be able to bear it" (1 Cor. 10:13).

9

What Practical Changes May I Expect in My Life After Sanctification?

At least three practical changes will be wrought in your life by sanctification.

1. Your life will be characterized by a simple faith. This is illustrated in the lives of two men filled with the Spirit at Pentecost, Peter and John. Each day a beggar was brought to the entrance of the Temple known as the "Gate Beautiful." In contrast to the beautiful gold and silver gate, I've pictured the man sitting there cross-legged in the dust, his shoulders stooped, eyes sunken, and the color had long since left his cheeks. The poor beggar was the last word in disconsolation.

On this day as he sat begging, his face lit up, for he saw coming two men whom he recognized as followers of Jesus. He said to himself, "They'll never let me down." Putting on his most pitiful plea he cried, "Have mercy on me. Give me a few coins, that I may buy a little bread." Peter and

John were moved with compassion; but as they felt about their cloaks, they realized they were penniless. However, these men had a simple faith which could not be equaled by silver and gold. The Scriptures don't record the prayer which no doubt they prayed. When they finished, Peter, who was always the spokesman of any group of which he was a member, began, "Silver and gold have I none; but such as I have give I thee: In the name of Jesus Christ of Nazareth rise up and walk."

As Peter assisted the man to his feet, the beggar suddenly realized that strength had come into those lifeless limbs. He began to rejoice, and ran into the Temple to tell the people of the miracle. Peter and John were short on silver and gold, but they had an abundance of "simple faith."

"The devil trembles when he sees the weakest saint upon his knees." I sometimes wonder how much he trembles when he sees some Christians upon their knees. Some of our prayers have been prayed for so long that they are little more than "vain repetition." Our Sunday school superintendent used to call on a man to lead in prayer who prayed the same prayer every week. He was so consistent that I could proceed a few words ahead of him in his weekly recitation. I'm sure those prayers never rose higher than the sound of his voice.

Praying in the Spirit involves more than words. Have you ever prayed with such concern that finally you fell across the bed crying, "O God, I know no more to say nor do. It is just in Your hands"? "Likewise the Spirit also helpeth our infirmities: for we know not what we should pray for as we ought: but the Spirit itself maketh intercession for us with groanings which cannot be uttered. . . . And we know that all things work together for good to them that love God" (Rom. 8:26, 28). The sanctified person learns to leave his life in the hands of God. He frets not, for his trust is in the Lord. He doesn't criticize, pout, nor get angry; for he knows that even the unfortunate things which happen in the church and in his private life will be worked out for the glory of God. No such abiding faith can be exerted by those not fully consecrated.

2. Your life will be characterized by a poised spirit. We see so few sweet-spirited people. Everyone is ready to stand for his rights. We blow our horns wildly at the fellow who interferes with our speed on the highway. And it seems that even some good people must, to put it blandly, occasionally "let off steam." At these times, words are spoken, scenes created, and decisions made which are later regretted. Often the good which has been built up over a period of years can be undone by one angry emotional upset. But Christ has power that will keep you with a right attitude even under pressure.

This is illustrated in the lives of two Spirit-filled men, Paul and Silas. As they taught and preached in the market place of Philippi, a young fortuneteller followed after them. She could tell people things about themselves which they already knew, but they would pay to hear her say it. Pointing to Paul and Silas, she said to the crowd, "These are men of God." Then Paul commanded that evil spirit to come out, and immediately she was pure.

Certain men who were her managers had been getting rich off her rantings. Though they cared little for her chastity, they did love the money she brought in. When she became pure, they at once became angry with Paul and Silas. The preachers were brought into court to answer a case fabricated by these men. With no semblance of a fair trial, their hands were tied above their heads in preparation for the administration of the Roman rods, the most cruel weapon of that era. Blood cascaded down their backs as the stripes were laid. Huge welts were raised where the skin was not broken. Their eyes became bloodshot, and their muscles ached under the strain. At last their hands were cut loose, to dangle like weights on the ends of lifeless cords at their sides. Brusquely, they were cast into the inner dungeon of the prison.

Here in the musty atmosphere of this vermin-infested cell they were fastened securely in the rough wooden stocks to await further punishment the next day. With no salve administered, the blood caked on their open wounds. Rats ran the rafters while guards stalked outside.

If they had been most modern Christians, they would have begun to complain. But Paul and Silas had an experience that held them steady in the darkest hour. At midnight, the Bible says, they began to sing and pray. It is not difficult to pray in the hour of testing, but it takes a good spirit to sing at such a time. Some Christians will scarcely sing in the enthusiasm of an evangelistic rally.

47

I don't know what they sang, but if it had been now, it might have been:

> *Must Jesus bear the cross alone,*
> *And all the world go free?*
> *No, there's a cross for everyone,*
> *And there's a cross for me.*

I don't know where you work, your homelife, nor the difficult persons with whom you have to deal; but I do know that the Lord has an experience that will hold you steady when the rest of the world is distraught.

3. Your life will be characterized with a dauntless courage for Christ. Peter illustrates this. He was a cowardly, overgrown, tousled-haired fisherman. During the trial of Christ at the hall of the high priest, a little girl severely frightened him when she called him a follower of Jesus. When the soldiers began to press the issue, he cursed and blasphemed to prove that he had never known the Savior.

But after the Day of Pentecost, where is Peter? He is not in some secluded desert hideaway but, rather, down in Jerusalem, in the center of hostilities. He is back in the city where Christ was arraigned and where His enemies are lurking at every corner. In this hostile center, Peter preached on street corners until his converts numbered 3,000.

This change in Peter was not the result of study in psychology, nor the outcome of a course in personal achievement. The difference was this: Peter had been filled with the Spirit.

I want to be charitable toward those individuals who find making conversation a difficult task, but I seriously doubt if a sanctified person can keep from witnessing for Christ.

In summary: Your sanctified life will be characterized by: (1) simple faith; (2) a poised spirit; and (3) a dauntless courage to witness for Christ.

10

How Do I Keep Sanctified?

Growth in grace is the only antidote to stagnation and backsliding. You are not sanctified to sit down and glide to heaven, but to live a life of service and to grow continually in the grace of God. Three simple rules which I've been applying in my life will work in yours.

1. Be absolutely sincere. You had to be absolutely sincere before you could ever be saved or sanctified. "Ye shall seek me, and find me, when ye shall search for me with your whole heart" (Jer. 29:13). The same thing it took to appropriate God's grace will be required to sustain it; we must be sincere.

No one knows how sincere you are except you and God. Your friends may have their opinion, but you and God alone know.

For instance: On Sunday morning your pastor will say, "Shall we all stand together and unite our hearts in the morning prayer." Everybody will stand and almost everyone will bow his head and close his eyes. If I were to look out across the congregation, I would naturally think, They are praying. But you well know that, even though congregation is standing in the posture of prayer, their minds may be 500 miles from the morning service. No one knows how sincere you are in that prayer except you and God.

This humorous story illustrates the point. Desiring the night off, a trombonist asked his brother to substitute for him. His scoffs were finally subdued with this plan: "A player will sit on either side of you. From the corner of your eyes, watch; then push and pull your slide just as they do." Finally, for a sizable monetary consideration, the brother consented to the deceptive plot. That night the conductor beat rhythm while the brazen mimic followed perfectly each movement of the slip-horn artists next to him. Everything went beautifully until they came to a solo passage for the trombone section, and it turned out that all three were substitutes and none could blow a note.

Sometimes, we almost reach such extremes in our worship. We can go through the Sunday morning service and at the dinner table scarcely recall a thought from the message.

In Oregon, where it rains a great deal, someone put up a sign on an unpaved road, "Pick out your rut, brother; you'll be in it for the next 20 miles." Some people, it seems, lag into a spiritual rut which brings no joy to themselves or others. Sincerity is absolutely necessary for growth in grace.

2. Then, you must have a complete coordination between your will and the will of God. Jesus set the example for us in His experience at the Garden of Gethsemane. His burden was so great that "bloody beads of perspiration" broke out on

His brow. Yonder, sleeping, were His most trusted disciples, whom He had left to watch. Henchmen from the office of the high priest were already en route to arrest Him. But he prayed: "O my Father, if it be possible, let this cup pass from me: nevertheless not as I will, but as thou wilt" (Matt. 26:39).

The artist who painted "The Last Supper," which they have in the stained-glass window at Forest Lawn Cemetery in California, has one hand of Christ turned down and the other turned up. In interpreting his work, the artist said that the hand turned down means, "If possible, let this cup pass"; but with the hand turned up Christ says, "Thy will be done."

Christ many times said, "I seek not my own will, but the will of him who hath sent me." In John's Gospel he said, "It is my meat to do the will of my Father in heaven." If you and I expect to grow in grace, we must have that same attitude, "a complete coordination between our will and the will of God."

When I first went to Oregon, I was taken by friends to visit the logging camps. My eyes bugged as I watched them cut the giant fir, trim it, haul it to the pond; and finally to see it come as shining straight lumber from the mill. I enjoyed every part of the process, but I was most interested in watching the long trucks haul the giant trees. One camp I visited was cutting pilings to be sent to Pearl Harbor. Some of them were 150 feet long and were hauled on special trucks. In the cab one driver steered the front of the truck, and back 50 feet another man with a separate apparatus guided the rear portion of the huge truck. They told me that some awful accidents occurred when the two drivers failed to turn in complete harmony. When the first man started around a treacherous mountain curve, the second man had to coordinate his actions; or, in a second, the truck was off the road, demolishing whatever it hit and oftentimes killing both drivers.

It is like that with our lives. Christ knows the way and will guide our lives in the right path, but we must cooperate by following His will. Many a person has wrecked his Christian life when he refused to follow the course of Christ.

During the last decade of the 19th century, a world's fair held in St. Louis, Missouri, exhibited the greatest collection of clocks in the world. The largest clock was there with a long hand that stretched out for 60 feet. The clock towered high above the grounds and could be seen for miles. At the base of the world's largest clock was a pedestal on which rested the world's smallest watch, a tiny Swiss model, smaller than a dime.

People would look at the little watch and then crane their necks to gaze at the large clock above, anxious to see if the indicated time was identical. Always there was complete coordination. When the huge clock said noon, so did the little watch. When the small watch pointed to three, so did the great clock in the tower. God is as the world's largest clock. None of us will ever equal Him, but each of us may have a complete coordination between our will and the will of God.

3. Then we must have "plain determination." When I attended elementary school, they had us

read about Theodore Roosevelt as an example in perseverance. Born frail, he could never play with the bigger boys. They always taunted him, "Run on, Skinny; you'll get hurt." Finally he took enough and demanded that his father help him build a body. The wealthy parents outfitted the youth with a gym, a teacher, and the necessary equipment. And young Roosevelt started out to build himself a body. You know the rest of the story. He became a ranger on the Western plains, head of the "Rough Riders" during the Spanish-American War, a president of the United States, and one of the greatest big-game hunters the world has known—all because of determination.

One night during the war, I was riding in the observation car on a train between New York and Chicago. The man in the chair adjoining mine arose, leaving a magazine, which I picked up and opened at random. I'm sure I'll never forget the true story that I read, written by an army doctor; here it is in essence.

During the war on a certain day when fighting was extraordinarily hard, the medical corps officer saw it was useless trying to attend each casualty. Finally he gave this order, "Men, you can't bring in everyone. Use your own judgment and help those who have a chance to live."

Two attendants coming across a foxhole saw a 19-year-old boy badly shot and nearly dead. They said to each other, "He doesn't have a chance to live. We'll leave him and go after someone else." Turning their backs on the dying boy, they started to leave. But even though the boy was more dead than alive he heard their conversation. Mustering all the power he could into his lips, throat, and vocal cords, he raised his head slightly and screamed, "I'm not going to die. I'm going to live. Won't you come back and help me?" Turning back, the men with the stretcher looked again on the helpless youth. "He wouldn't live until we got him to first aid," they said. "We've got to leave him. It's orders." Once more they turned to go, and again the lad screamed. As they looked on him the third time one said, "After all, it's his last request. I guess if we were in his place we'd want this done for us." So, placing his mangled form on the stretcher, they started for the first-aid station. As they walked through the entrance, the boy was still alive. Looking up into the doctor's face, he blurted, "I'm not going to die. I'm going to live, and I'm going back to finish this war." The doctor, who authored the article, confessed that after the boy went by he shook his head and said inwardly, "He doesn't have a chance in a thousand."

The youngster had so much spunk that they gave him a shot in the arm and a nurse began cleaning the wounds. To shorten the story: at the end of three months the boy walked out of an army hospital under his own power, with the aid of a pair of crutches. The physician closed the very dramatic article by saying, "There is only one thing that saved that boy's life, and that was pure determination."

Closing the magazine, I tossed it back into the chair, and bowed my head while I prayed a prayer many miles long that night as we sped across the rails. "O Lord, help me to have determination; determination to resist sin, to resist temptation, to resist those things which would drag me down in my Christian experience. Help me to have determination to keep my eyes off people and situations, and to keep them upon Christ."

Our only hope to keep sanctified is to grow in grace, be sincere, follow God's will, and practice determination.